974.965
pb

Smith, Richard S.

Images of America, Princeton

	DATE DUE		
6/21/01			
AUG. 29 2001			
OCT. 9 1 2001			
JUL. 22 2002			
FEB 1 2 2006			

Town and gown are shown in this aerial photo from the 1950s, with Princeton's business district to the north (left) of Nassau Street, the town's main thoroughfare, and the university campus to the south (right). (Courtesy of Princeton Pictorial Archive.)

IMAGES
of America

PRINCETON

Richard D. Smith

ARCADIA

First published 1997
Copyright © Richard D. Smith, 1997

ISBN 0-7524-0586-1

Published by Arcadia Publishing,
an imprint of the Chalford Publishing Corporation,
One Washington Center, Dover, New Hampshire 03820.
Printed in Great Britain

Library of Congress Cataloging-in-Publication Data applied for

This book is dedicated to Constance M. Greiff,
architectural historian and a mainstay of the Historical Society of Princeton,
and to her husband, Robert,
with best wishes.

Contents

Acknowledgments   6

Introduction   7

1.   Princeton's Beginnings, America's Beginnings   9

2.   A Busy Borough   21

3.   Education (Including a Certain Famous University)   39

4.   An International Community   57

5.   Homes Humble and Grand   65

6.   Getting About   75

7.   Life and Leisure   85

8.   Worship   101

9.   The Famous and Influential   109

10.   Research and Much Development   119

Acknowledgments

Princeton is a fascinating place because of its wonderful inhabitants, not just because of its well-documented history. Similarly, *Images of America: Princeton* reflects the interest of numerous persons and not just the work of its credited author. Many thanks, therefore, go to the Historical Society of Princeton for its cooperation in making this book possible (all photographs, unless otherwise credited, are from the society's outstanding collection) and especially to director Gail Stern and recent publication committee chairperson Nancy B. Eills, for their enthusiastic facilitation of the process; to society staff members Maureen M. Smyth and Jane L. Rudes, for their sunny assistance; to Winnie Okamitsu and Mary-Peale Schofield, my two absolutely superb research assistants; to Arcadia Publishing editor Jamie Carter, for her easy-going professionalism; and to all the wonderful persons and groups who generously contributed additional images.

I relied heavily on many published sources for general information and specific tidbits, notably *Princeton Architecture* by Constance M. Greiff, Mary W. Gibbons, and Elizabeth G.C. Menzies; *Princeton: On The Streets Where We Live* by Randy Hobler and Jeanne Silvester; and back issues of *The Princeton Recollector*, edited by Elric J. Endersby (whose Princeton Pictorial Archive has also been the source for several important photos). Unpublished notes on the Historical Society's photo collection by Wanda S. Gunning were also extremely valuable. Connie Greiff and Wanda Gunning possess encyclopedic knowledge about Princeton history, and I am confident that their meticulous reviews of the manuscript have rendered it as error free as humanly possible.

Introduction

"Princeton is a wonderful little spot, a quaint and ceremonious village."
—Albert Einstein, letter to Queen Elizabeth of Belgium, November 20, 1933.

The great physicist who became Princeton's most famous resident had been in town less than a month when he expressed those sentiments. Yet Einstein, who provided revolutionary insights into the nature of time and space, might have known that people from the receding past had also deeply loved this place. In 1766, Richard Stockton, master of the estate called Morven, forebear of an old Princeton family, and a signer of the Declaration of Independence, wrote from London to his wife, Annis, that he would rather walk "along the rivulets of Morven . . . and see the rural sports of the chaste little frogs" than attend the Queen's ball.

Princeton's charms are obvious, but if there is a key to understanding the town it is that the more things change here, the more they remain the same. Princeton was an important stop along early transportation routes, and it quickly became a seat of learning and communications in Colonial times. Today's bustling Route One business corridor just outside Princeton is merely the inheritor of that tradition. Princeton was a settlement where small groups of varied nationalities became established and made homes. Such is its ethnic history to this very day.

The famous have come to live and work here, the famous keep coming. As the town grows, its builders often find it better to move and reuse structures rather than tear them down, a Princeton practice that actually goes back nearly two centuries. Throughout its history, Princeton has succeeded in being modern and efficient, and traditional and timeless, all at once. The wonderful thing is that the meeting edges of such contrasts are virtually seamless, with no dissonance or unworkable contradiction.

Princeton is in many ways like a New England village. In some ways it is like a Southern town. And in the best ways it represents the spirit of New Jersey: the proud, historically significant former colony and geographically diverse state which has, sadly, replaced Brooklyn, New York, as the butt of cheap jokes by aspiring comedians. The beautiful borough of Princeton and the charming countryside of surrounding Princeton Township—and the loveliness of locales like them from the hilly splendor of High Point to the vibrant Victoriana of Cape May—give the lie to the stereotype of New Jersey as an esthetic wasteland of oil refineries, grungy cities, and suburban sprawl. Ironically, Princeton represents the best of the state so well that it is often dismissed with another stereotype; that it is an enclave of rich, effete snobs. Although the wealthy and internationally famous are well represented here, Princeton is in fact a socially, economically, and ethnically diverse community. And as *Images of America: Princeton* clearly proves through the documentary evidence of historic photographs, it has been this way for many, many years.

One
Princeton's Beginnings, America's Beginnings

This 1764 engraving by William Tennent provides an early view of Nassau Hall (with the college president's home to the right) at Princeton University, then known as the College of New Jersey. First occupied in November 1756, the hall housed the entire school and was the largest stone building in America. It was almost named Belcher Hall after New Jersey's governor. Fortunately, Jonathan Belcher suggested that King William III and the House of Nassau be honored instead.

An "Especially Agreeable" Place

Is Princeton real estate so expensive today because for millions of years it was beachfront property? Princeton is at the edge of a great natural divide: to the southeast (just beyond today's U.S. Highway One) begins the flat sandy terrain that eventually leads to the Pine Barrens and which was created by the ebb and flow of prehistoric oceans; immediately to the northwest of town (beyond state road 206) begins the gently rolling countryside leading to the Sourland Mountains, ancient hills which are geologically a northern extension of the Appalachians.

The town's pleasant location was remarked on by early visitors. Wrote a traveler from Germany in 1783: "Princeton is a little country town of only one considerable street in which few houses stand, but its elevated site makes the place especially agreeable, the view from it being splendid, out over the lower country as far as Neversinks [Navesink, near the Jersey shore] and other parts of the coast." It is a picturesque and altogether fitting setting for a town that is rich in history and has often been in the vanguard of the future.

Princeton once lay along another boundary, that of the 1676 division of the state into West and East Jerseys between two groups of proprietors who held the land and administered it. An attempt in 1687 to survey a boundary between the two got off course and was abandoned but left the legacy of the long straight byway west of town called Province Line Road. A second, successful land survey in 1743 moved the line many miles to the east, placing Princeton in the domain of West Jersey. (In 1702, beset by problems with unruly settlers, the land companies returned civil authority to the British crown, resulting in the single colony of New Jersey.)

The first Princetonians were probably American Indians of the Delaware tribe, specifically the group that has been termed the Lenni Lenape, a Delaware phrase meaning "the original people." Although no sites of major, long-term habitation have been discovered in the immediate vicinity of Princeton, there is evidence that the Delawares hunted in the area and lived in small family groups along Stony Brook. Important local roads may have begun as Indian trails through the dense woodlands, the primary growth forest which later became farmland, cattle pastures, and orchards under the Europeans.

The story of European-American settlement in Princeton really begins in 1696, when land grants were made to about a half-dozen families, most of whom were members of the Society of Friends. They established their farms and their meeting house near the banks of Stony Brook, about two miles west of what is now downtown Princeton, in a region known to the Native Americans as Wapowog. Thus the settlement's first name was Stony Brook.

But by 1724, the name Prince Town had come into usage. There was actually a string of royal nomenclature. Northeast along the stagecoach road was Queens Town. Located around the intersection of what are now Nassau and Harrison Streets, Queens Town became known as Jugtown because of an active pottery business that operated into the 1850s. It was finally subsumed by Princeton's growth. There was also a Kings Town further to the northeast, now called Kingston. And yes, on the other side of Princeton, there was a Princessville, but today a small cemetery on Princeton Pike just over the Lawrence Township line is all that remains of a hamlet once known for its Methodist Episcopal Church and a tavern that catered to stagecoach passengers and cattle drovers.

During the War of Independence, Princeton was the site of a battle small in size but immense in significance. After their famous crossing of the Delaware River on Christmas 1776 and subsequent capture of Trenton, George Washington and his army successfully fended off the British during a second battle of Trenton. By the time British reinforcements arrived on January 3, 1777, to push the Continentals into the river and crush the revolt, Washington had slipped away by night and taken back roads to Princeton. The Americans defeated a detachment of British west of town (at a site preserved today as the Princeton Battlefield Park) and escaped north to Morristown, New Jersey, to camp for the rest of the winter. Washington's third victory in ten days not only revived his enlisted men's spirits, but caused the crowned heads of Europe and dissident members of Parliament to voice the unthinkable—that the war would not be a short one and that Britain might not even win.

The college at Princeton suffered looting during the struggle and a terrible financial crisis afterwards. But from late June to early November 1783, it became the de facto capitol of the United States when Congress, facing a possible coup by restless, unpaid soldiers, quietly left Philadelphia and resumed their deliberations in Nassau Hall. Washington arrived in August to lend his authority to the proceedings. He stayed at Rockingham, a property at nearby Rocky Hill, where he entertained old comrades, wrote his farewell address to the army, and posed for the portrait on page 17. Rockingham is today a state historic house open to the public. Local property owners leased rooms to the visiting delegates. On October 31, 1783, these delegates received word that the Treaty of Paris had been signed. The War of Independence had been successful. America and Princeton were about to come into their own.

The stone meetinghouse of the Society of Friends (Quakers) at Stony Brook was completed in 1724 and rebuilt after a fire in December 1759. This photo from the 1880s shows the building and bordering farmland much as they would have appeared on January 3, 1777, when the Battle of Princeton was fought a scant half mile away.

Washington's men tore up planking from the wooden bridge over Stony Brook to slow British troops returning to Princeton from Trenton on the King's Highway. The span that replaced it in 1792 still carries traffic and is one of the oldest stone arch bridges in America. The adjacent Worth's Mill operated from around 1714 until the early twentieth century, but only one wall survives.

The west wing of Morven was built around 1755 for Richard Stockton (1730–1781), a signer of the Declaration of Independence and scion of a family whose descendants still live in Princeton. Significantly expanded in the nineteenth century, Morven was for many years the official residence of New Jersey's governors.

Annis Boudinot Stockton (1736–1801) was the witty and energetic wife of signer Stockton and sister of Elias Boudinot, president of the Continental Congress. A capable estate manager and popular hostess, she was also an engaging poet. An unknown artist has depicted her holding a sprig of myrtle, a flower associated with poetic inspiration. (Courtesy of the Art Museum, Princeton University: Gift of Mr. and Mrs. Landon K. Thorne for the Boudinot Collection.)

The formidable Scottish cleric John Witherspoon (1723–1794) headed the college at Princeton from 1768 until his death. A signer of the Declaration, he warned that America was not only ripe for independence, but "in danger of rotting for the want of it." The road he traveled from Nassau Hall to his farm Tusculum outside town was named Witherspoon Street in his honor.

This house at the intersection of Nassau and Harrison, in what was once the community of Queens Town, may have been built as early as 1730 by the Scott family and was probably rented to members of the Continental Congress meeting in Princeton in 1783. When Harrison Street was widened, the wing on the right was moved to the building's opposite side.

On July 29, 1812, Dr. Archibald Alexander, sole professor at the newly created Princeton Theological Seminary, "removed my family to this place, where a house was provided for us, not very large or commodious, but the best which could be obtained." This quaint early-nineteenth-century structure served as the seminary's first meeting place and now stands, greatly modified, at 134 Mercer Street.

An early wing of The Barracks on Edgehill Street was home to Richard Stockton, grandfather of the signer of the Declaration, who bought the land in 1696. The earliest construction may have been by prior property owner Daniel Brinson after 1686. Edgehill Street is also one of Princeton's oldest streets, originally a lane leading to Stockton's door. Tradition has it that soldiers were barracked in the home during the French and Indian War.

Just after dawn on January 3, 1777, British troops left Princeton to join what was expected to be the third and decisive battle of Trenton. Surprised by the glint of sunlight on bayonets moving in the opposite direction, they rushed to investigate and encountered soldiers of the Continental Army, which had slipped out of Trenton by back roads during the night. The Battle of Princeton soon took place on the properties of Quaker farmers William and Thomas Clarke, a site shown here in an 1851 artist's conception. (Courtesy of Princeton Pictorial Archive.)

Although outnumbered, the Redcoats began routing the Americans. At the risk of his life, Washington rode into the thick of the battle and called out, "Parade with us, my brave fellows! There is but a handful of the enemy, and we shall have them directly." Thus rallied, the Continentals swept the field, later capturing many British soldiers at Nassau Hall after a brief firefight. In "Washington at Princeton," artist Charles Wilson Peale has depicted American general Hugh Mercer (on the right) lying mortally wounded. (Courtesy of Princeton University.)

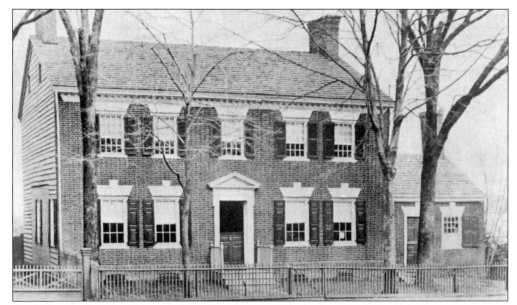

Built by prosperous tanner Job Stockton in the 1760s, the well-preserved, mid-Georgian brick house at 158 Nassau Street is called Bainbridge House in honor of Commodore William Bainbridge, commander of the USS *Constitution* ("Old Ironsides") during the War of 1812, who was born here. Shown in an 1875 photograph, it was a boarding house for university students at the turn of the century, served as the public library from 1910 to 1967, and is now home to the Historical Society of Princeton.

Absalom Bainbridge, the commodore's father, and Ebenezer Stockton, a later occupant, were physicians. This re-creation of a late-eighteenth-century doctor's office with period remedies and equipment was a popular Historical Society exhibit for many years.

This rare view of Witherspoon Street looking toward Nassau Hall was probably taken around or slightly after the Civil War, but shows how Princeton might have looked at the end of the 1700s, when it was a village of about one hundred homes.

This old inn stood at the northeast corner of Nassau and Witherspoon Streets, and in its time was a busy stagecoach stop. It was torn down and replaced in 1896 by the Tudor Revival-style building called Lower Pyne (see page 24). The inn is shown here in October 1881, a decade and a half before its removal, a relic of the good-old Colonial days.

A week's stay in Princeton in September 1847 was documented in the sketchbook of Lewis Miller of York, Pennsylvania, who visited his nephew Charles Miller, a student at the seminary. The elder Miller heard "a good sermon" preached on Sunday and also found a local "botanic garden . . . well worthy of a visit." (Courtesy of York County Historical Society.)

Two

A Busy Borough

This is a view down Nassau Street looking west, circa 1861. During the nineteenth century, Princeton's main thoroughfare was dusty when dry and mucky when wet. The original Nassau Inn (center, behind the oval sign), built prior to 1757, hosted travelers on the New York to Philadelphia stage line. It was torn down in 1937 to make way for Palmer Square.

Prospering Princeton

Nassau Street, the town's main thoroughfare and the lifeline of its business district, was a bustling byway even before there was a Princeton. It was probably at one time a section of the Assunpink Indian Trail which transversed what would become New Jersey, thus making Nassau Street one of the oldest continually used byways in the United States. The trail was widened into what became known as the Post Road and the King's Highway. It was, of course, a primary stagecoach road in the eighteenth and nineteenth centuries, and Princeton prospered as a stop along it. In the twentieth century, Nassau Street was a link in the Lincoln Highway (the first trans-American throughroad in the days before the interstates) and is now officially part of Route 27. Like Nassau Hall, Princeton University's original main building, the street was named in honor of William of the House of Orange-Nassau, later King of England.

Princeton Borough, essentially the downtown area, was incorporated by act of the state legislature on February 11, 1813. Princeton had only about seven hundred residents at that time, but was situated on the dividing line between Middlesex and Somerset Counties. A major impetus behind creation of the borough was that law enforcement officers needed a single jurisdiction and their own local jail so they would not have to transport prisoners—including rowdy revelers who flocked to town during college commencements—to the county seats in New Brunswick or Somerville. Princeton became part of Middlesex. Mercer County, where Princeton is now located, was created in 1838. Princeton Township, which surrounds the borough, was created in the same year and to date remains a separate entity, although the two Princetons now share many municipal services.

By 1850, according to census figures, 33.8% of occupations in the Princeton area were taken up in small businesses or skilled trades, 7.1% in professional careers, and 10.2% in running a farm, with 48.8% working as farm laborers, servants, or common laborers. There was still widespread farming and gardening, however, and one admiring visitor noted the bountiful fruit trees and "the orchards laden with fruit to admiration. Their very limbs [are] torn to pieces with the weight."

The growth of the town and its business district was boosted in the 1830s by the opening of the nearby Delaware & Raritan Canal. The Princeton Basin district at the southern end of Canal Street was filled out with stores, hotels, manufacturing facilities, and other businesses. The railroad further improved the region's fortunes, although it eventually put an end to Princeton Basin and mercantile activities along the canal (see pages 78 and 79). Canal Street was subsequently renamed Alexander Street in honor of Dr. Archibald Alexander, a professor at the Princeton Theological Seminary.

Meanwhile, the business district began to expand on Nassau Street and adjacent lanes. College students shopped not only for clothing in town (and occasionally pawned extra duds to finance recreational jaunts to New York!), but also rented rooms above the stores. Major family enterprises were founded in the nineteenth century. For example, Frederick William Luttmann's harness makers shop was the progenitor of Luttmann's Luggage, a successful Princeton luggage and leather goods specialty store. African Americans made up about 20% of Princeton's population by the mid-nineteenth century and were at first largely manual laborers, some finding employment as menial workers at the college. But black-owned businesses arose, some catering to the African-American community around Witherspoon Street, a few others successfully serving a white clientele. In the late nineteenth and early twentieth centuries, Italian immigrants found work as stonemasons, quarrymen, and groundskeepers; and soon their countrymen founded such successful local enterprises as Zazzali's Bakery in 1895, Toto's Market in 1912, and Caruso's tailor shop in 1917.

There really were quarries on Quarry Street and Quarry Lane (the latter owned by the Matthews Construction Company which built many of the university's great Collegiate Gothic structures, notably the university chapel). The Queens Town district, situated around the intersection of Nassau and Harrison Streets and soon to be annexed by an expanding Princeton, became widely known as Jug Town, due to the busy pottery production operation there. No less busy, but more odoriferous, were the tanneries on Moore Street and slaughterhouses at the north end of Witherspoon Street.

The opening in 1954 of the Princeton Shopping Center on Harrison Street in Princeton Township caused considerable anxiety among the merchants in the borough, but their continued personal service maintained sufficient customer loyalty so that the downtown district did not overly suffer. A similar easygoing atmosphere has helped the shopping center four decades later to survive the challenges of the great regional shopping malls. In business, as in the town itself, smaller and slightly old-fashioned can be better.

While financier and university trustee Moses Taylor Pyne was encouraging the rebuilding of the campus in Collegiate Gothic, he tried to reinvent Princeton's main thoroughfare as the high street of an English village. In 1896 he commissioned two Tudor Revival buildings on Nassau Street. Lower Pyne still stands at the corner of Witherspoon.

Upper Pyne was built at 74–76 Nassau. It inspired Charles V. Gulick, owner of this adjacent property at 72 Nassau, to redo Myron E. La Vake's jewelry store and the entry to Baker's Alley in the same style. The fate of picturesque Upper Pyne is documented on pages 126–127.

The Farr Hardware Company at the angular intersection of Nassau and Mercer called itself, quite literally, "The Corner Store." Harry Farr carried not only housewares, but sold agricultural implements to township farmers and was the "Headquarters for Lawn and Garden Seeds."

Meanwhile, Zapf's Hardware at 118 Nassau promoted lawn mowers and other items for property upkeep, evidently catering to the growing number of borough homeowners. Charles Zapf often displayed his goods on the sidewalk beneath a wood canopy. (Courtesy of Princeton Pictorial Archive.)

Opened in 1878, Joseph Priest's pharmacy was one of the town's leading drugstores. In October 1914, the building was moved back 60 feet to make room for a proposed war memorial. (The little "French Market" eventually occupied the emptied site.) The building is now home to the *Town Topics* newspaper.

The Kingston Roller Mill was owned by Nelson Thompson & Co., which in 1910 advertised five grades of deliciously named flours ("White Star," "Golden Wing," "Seal," "Purity," and "Matchless") and animal feeds of all kinds. "Our machinery is modern—We produce superior flour[s], clean and nourishing—They will please you." This mill building is the only one still standing along the Millstone River. (Courtesy of Princeton Pictorial Archive.)

The J.V. Lemming store stood on the southeast corner of Nassau and Harrison Streets in the old Queens Town/Jugtown district. Built in the 1830s, it was for many years a tavern. Lemming bought it around 1880 from its owners, the Margerum family, and established the store.

The old borough jail was located at the corner of what is now Hulfish Street and Palmer Square West. William Leggett, town marshal in the late 1800s, was at 6 feet and 230 pounds a formidable upholder of law and order. Declared one guest of this stark establishment: "If I'd have knowed I was in Princeton, I wouldn't have got drunk. The Marshall of Princeton is known as far as the Rio Grande."

As new residences were built around town, much of the demand for hardware, plumbing, and gas fittings was met by McCreavor & Whyte at 36 Alexander Street. Their firm was the successor to the business of tinsmith Samuel M. Ross at the same address.

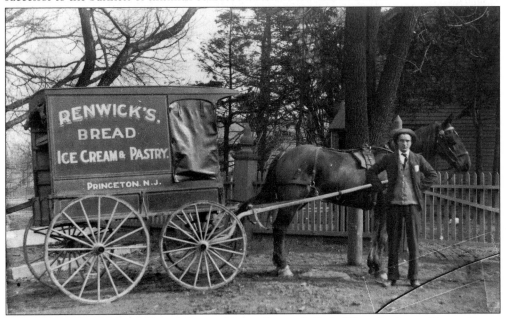

John Renwick not only sold bread; Renwick's Ice Cream & Soda Water Parlor on Nassau Street was a Princeton institution well into the 1960s.

Grocer and flavoring maker W.W. Leggett (see page 32) was also the local agent for Chase motor vehicles in 1910, so it's no surprise to find his Princeton Brand Extracts being distributed from a Chase truck. At the wheel is Charles A. LaTourette, future editor-publisher of the *Princeton Packet* newspaper.

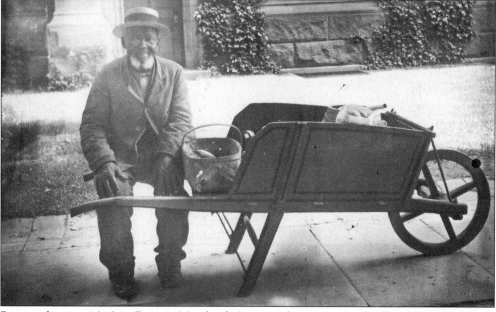

Born a slave in 1816 in Easton, Maryland, Jimmy Johnson was a childhood friend of black abolitionist Frederick Douglass. He escaped to Princeton in 1839 where his freedom was purchased by sympathetic white residents. Shown here around 1890, he worked as a janitor, then ran a used clothing store, and finally sold apples, nuts, and lemonade—nineteenth-century fast food—to college students from his famous wheelbarrow.

This is a view of Spring Street looking toward Vandeventer Avenue. That's right, there was once a spring-fed pond in downtown Princeton. Covered over in 1898, the spring now runs underground, gurgling in the street's storm drains. Beatty House (background, center) was moved in 1877 from its Nassau Street location to what would become Vandeventer, named after the family who operated a tree nursery on the land.

This large garden was grown by the Ulyat family at 93 Alexander Street *c*. 1915. Today a golf course preserves much of the open space around the Princeton University graduate school (background) with its magnificent Grover Cleveland memorial tower.

A stone crushing operation plus 87 acres of fruit trees and vegetables provided work at the township poor farm. Founded in 1842 as the Mount Lucas Orphan and Guardian Institute, New Jersey's first orphanage, it eventually became a Princeton Township institution for adults and operated well into the 1920s. John Hageman, a nineteenth-century local historian, noted that with the farm's establishment "the community has been agreeably relieved from the annoyance of excessive begging."

In the days before electric refrigerators, block ice was an important product. The Princeton Ice Company's operations near Mountain Avenue produced "Natural Ice From Pure Spring Water." Today, concrete and brick remains of the company's buildings can be seen along a popular hiking trail that winds through Princeton Community Park North to the Mountain Lakes property.

W.W. Leggett (center, with vest and watch chain) poses in front of his store at 120 Nassau Street. Leggett developed the successful line of "Princeton Brand" extracts ("The Extract with a Flavor"), his vanilla being particularly popular. As you can see, trading stamps that could be exchanged for premiums were a promotional device in American groceries decades before the "green stamps" craze of the 1950s.

Employees and a supervisor pose with the mighty belt-driven washing machines of the University Laundry Company at 28–30 Moore Street in 1904. Although not affiliated with Princeton University, the name of the business suggests its large college clientele. The company's horse-drawn wagons made daily pickups and deliveries.

Frank L. Krespach's Upholstery Shop is pictured here, c. 1898. Re-upholstering and repair of antique furniture was a specialty; so was patriotism during the days of the Spanish-American War.

Edward C. Kopp's establishment at 60–62 Nassau operated in the days before pre-made suits, with a tailor visiting twice weekly to take measurements and orders. But Kopp's Princeton immortality is due to the bicycle store he opened in 1888, which continues to this day under his name. Note the shoe repair shop under the steps: such basement businesses have all but vanished on Nassau Street.

Christine Moore Howell was not only a Paris-trained beautician, but an entrepreneur with a successful line of cosmetics and accessories. Shown standing in the 1920s in front of her beauty parlor at 12 Spring Street (with her sister Bessie, sitting), she authored the book *Beauty Culture and Care of the Hair*, was listed in *Who's Who in Colored America*, and became the first African American appointed to the New Jersey Board of Beauty Culture Control. (Courtesy of Donald Moore.)

The Vogel Brothers, Isaac and William, proudly display their wares to appreciative (and warmly furred) customers at their butcher shop at 104 Nassau Street in March 1936. (Courtesy of Princeton Pictorial Archive.)

In 1920, a small corner of the Lower Pyne building was quite sufficient for postmaster Benjamin H. Mount. A lovely 1930s-era post office still operates on Palmer Square, but Princeton's main branch is now a 35,800-square foot building physically located in neighboring West Windsor, handling 180,000 pieces of mail daily.

This telephone exchange (probably the Bell Telephone Company installation at 32 Nassau Street around 1910) was state-of-the-art for its time and anticipated Princeton's modern role as a communications center. Note that the operators are men, as was usually the case in the industry's early days.

The Princeton Bank & Trust building stands on the corner of Nassau and (fittingly enough) Bank Street. Organized in 1834, the bank was able to boast by 1910 of capital and undivided profits of $220,000. This 1897 structure is a lovely example of Dutch Revival architecture, and it still houses financial companies, although the bank has moved elsewhere. (Courtesy of Princeton Pictorial Archive.)

An early-twentieth-century photograph shows an eastward view of Nassau Street. Holder Hall's tower on the university campus (right) still defines the town's quaint skyline. Despite many horse-drawn conveyances, the "Fire Proof Garage" being advertised at No. 2 Nassau Street (left) reveals that the age of the motorcar has begun.

All Princeton mourned January 18, 1963, when the Baltimore Dairy Lunch—a.k.a. "The Balt"—took down its sign at 82 Nassau Street after forty years of operation. College students staged a funeral procession to its congenial counter, and one patron wrote in tribute, "Sing praises to a hamburger, a creamy chocolate malt/ Sing praises to the place we loved so well/ And shed a tear to the memory of the Balt."

Photographed in 1936 on the steps of the Jacob Lutz home at 12 Harrison Street, but recalled today only as "The Horseradish Man," this peddler went door to door grinding fresh supplies of the eye-watering condiment and grating coconut as a sideline. Peddlers competed with family-owned groceries that filled orders by telephone, allowed running accounts, and made deliveries. But both were challenged by post-World War Two automobile-driven mobility that steered customers to the new supermarkets. (Courtesy of Princeton Pictorial Archive.)

Three
Education
(Including a Certain Famous University)

Mary Louise Snook poses with her charges at the one-room Stony Brook School in 1904. Affectionately called "Miss Louie" and "Miss Snooks," she taught eight racially integrated grades, made sure that any child with vision or hearing problems sat up front, and at lunch time in winter let students skate on a nearby pond.

Local Learning

Think of Princeton and you may think of Princeton University, which is by no means the only place of higher learning in town, nor was it always known as "Princeton," nor was it founded here. And the town has been home to several other nationally and internationally known seats of higher learning, as well as many excellent public and private primary and secondary schools.

The College of New Jersey was chartered in 1746 in Elizabeth, where its first president and professor Jonathan Dickinson taught about ten students. The following year it relocated to Newark, but there was agitation to move it to a more central location in the state (and one without northeastern New Jersey's ubiquitous marshlands or ferocious mosquitoes). The colleges trustees demanded that any new home town provide an endowment of 1,000 pounds, 10 acres of cleared land for a campus, and 200 wooded acres to insure a supply of firewood. Princeton succeeded in attracting the college in 1756 when landowners Nathaniel FitzRandolph, John Stockton, Thomas Leonard, and their wives, plus John Hornor, deeded the necessary lands and contributed the money. These benefactors were enthusiastic about luring such a seat of higher learning to their town (and doubtless looked forward to an accompanying rise in commerce and property values). The college, in turn, began attracting students from as far away as the South and the West Indies.

Enrollment reached 314 by the time of the Civil War, about half the students being from below the Mason-Dixon line. Some wags dubbed the College of New Jersey "the northernmost southern school," and it did have the advantage of being closer to Virginia and Georgia than rivals Yale or Harvard. Postwar poverty (and perhaps bitterness) initially kept many Southern families from again sending their sons to the North for an education. But by 1896, the student body topped 1,200. The College of New Jersey began offering graduate studies and was renamed Princeton University.

Under the leadership of James McCosh, Woodrow Wilson, and other dedicated college presidents, Princeton University evolved into one of the finest schools in the world. It now has enrollments of approximately 4,500 undergraduates and 1,600 graduate students, working on a 600-acre campus whose 160 buildings contain more than 5.5 million square feet of space. To list all of Princeton's famous and successful alumni and faculty would require a telephone book-sized tome. Two graduates who should be mentioned are two U.S. presidents: James Madison, Class of 1771, who as a student complained that the town was "overstocked with old maids"; and Woodrow

Wilson, Class of 1879, who later served as a professor, the university's president, and New Jersey's governor before leading our nation through the trauma of World War I.

Two local schools are renowned for music studies. The Westminster Choir was founded by John Finley Williamson in Dayton, Ohio, in 1926 and moved three years later to Ithaca, New York. It came to Princeton in 1932, added graduate courses, and in 1939 became Westminster Choir College. (Today, it remains located in Princeton but is part of Lawrence Township-based Rider University.) Another leading music center came to the area when Williamson persuaded protégé Herbert Huffman to move Huffman's boychoir school from Columbus, Ohio, to Princeton. In 1950, the school acquired Albemarle, the Princeton estate of Gerald Lambert (manufacturer of Listerine-brand mouthwash), as its new home. Renamed the American Boychoir School in 1980, its student choir tours America and the world to great acclaim.

Other prominent centers of higher learning include the Princeton Theological Seminary, opened in 1812 in part because the Presbyterian General Assembly felt that the College of New Jersey's curriculum had become too secular for aspiring ministers. Today the seminary offers an ecumenical range of studies, is home to some of the world's most prominent biblical scholars, and has a superb collection of biblical manuscripts among its holdings. Evelyn College was a promising women's school. Established in 1887 by the Rev. Joshua Hall McIlvaine, a former Princeton college professor, and named in honor of seventeenth-century scholar Sir John Evelyn, it attracted many daughters of the Princeton faculty and sisters of its undergraduates. But in 1897 fund-raising difficulties and the death of president McIlvaine ended what might have become Princeton's answer to Radcliffe or Vassar. Its main building, "The Pines," was known locally as "the Christmas tree house" because it was painted green and red. It still stands, as a residence, at the end of Evelyn Place.

In addition to a fine public high school, Princeton has had many successful private secondary schools. Miss Fine's became the towns premiere girls' school, eventually merging with the Princeton Country Day boys' school to form the coed Princeton Day School. In 1914 John Gale Hun, a mathematics teacher, started a successful remedial instruction business that helped struggling undergraduates stay in Princeton. But in 1942 the university forbade students from taking commercial tutoring. Hun responded by founding the private secondary school which bears his name and occupies the former Russell estate just west of town. Across the Great Road from Princeton Day School is Stuart Country Day School of the Sacred Heart, a popular Catholic day school for girls. (Incidentally, the S.A.T.s taken by college-bound American high schoolers have a local origin: Educational Testing Service, now headquartered in nearby Lawrence Township, was founded in Princeton.)

Rivaling Princeton University as a prestigious academic center is the Institute for Advanced Study, whose campus is on Olden Lane in the southwest edge of town. Conceived in 1930 as a center where great scholars could continue their research at the highest levels, it was funded through the generosity of Louis Bamberger and his sister, Caroline Bamberger Fuld. One of the first faculty members recruited by organizer Abraham Flexner was Albert Einstein, who resigned his academic positions in Germany after the Nazis burned his books; he arrived in Princeton in October 1933. Einstein's presence helped to draw other intellectual émigrés. (Einstein was quick with letters of recommendation to help scholars fleeing the looming European conflagration gain entry into the United States.) Princeton's status as a world center for physics and advanced mathematics was secured.

Mt. Lucas School was built in 1874 as a "large, modern schoolhouse," but a former student recalled, "It was cold as the devil when you went in the morning because the fire was banked at night, and we had to start it going again." This and other one-room schools were closed in 1918 with the opening of the Township Consolidated School on Witherspoon Street.

Despite its grandiloquent name, the Princeton Model School was a public institution and a forerunner of Princeton High School. The motto of the class of 1882, shown here, was "Labor Omnia Vincit" ("Work Conquers All"). (Courtesy of Princeton Pictorial Archive.)

Grade-school children get a round of learning at the Nassau Street School. The building at 185 Nassau is now home to Princeton University art and theater classes.

St. Paul's Roman Catholic school students and teachers pose *c.* 1910. The parochial day school was started in the 1850s and for a time met in the church rectory. In 1880, its first separate building was erected.

Princeton Prep was founded in 1873 as an adjunct to the College of New Jersey. But the college divested itself of the school in the 1880s due to financial difficulties. Princeton Prep later flourished in private hands by stressing individual attention at each boy's learning level and offered a healthy athletic program, but finally closed in 1936 due to lingering effects of the Depression.

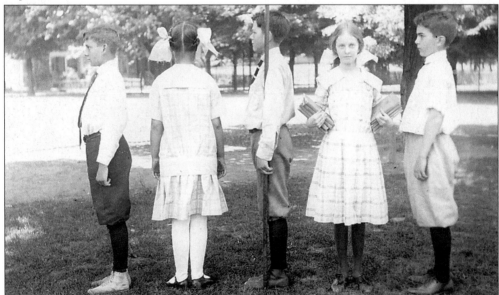

A vital regimen in late nineteenth- and early-twentieth-century grade schools was the teaching of good posture. These unidentified youngsters demonstrate lessons well learned about straight spines and beautiful balance.

May Margaret Fine, sister of Princeton Prep headmaster John Burchard Fine, founded her own private school around 1899. These 1919 Maypole dancers may have been students at Miss Fine's, which began coed but became a girls' school in the 1930s.

Princeton High School's vitality in creative arts goes back many decades. On February 23, 1917, the play *Crowning of the Gypsy Queen* was presented. In this spellbinding (or spell-casting?) moment, a witch foretells woe for the title character, intoning, "The caldron boils and bubbles, nor thinks of mortal troubles." (Courtesy of Princeton Pictorial Archive.)

The students at Evelyn College were taught a challenging curriculum of mathematics, science, art, and the classics by founder Joshua Hall McIlvaine (center) and his faculty. The institution's sunny, well-ventilated rooms and healthful surroundings enabled administrators to declare in 1891 that "during the four years' life of Evelyn College, a case of serious illness among the students has been unknown."

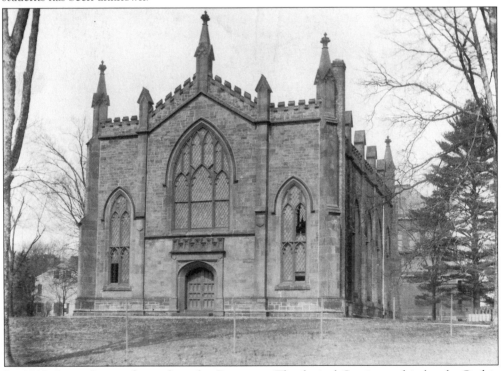

In 1843, James Lenox donated to the Princeton Theological Seminary this lovely Gothic Revival building to house the school's collection of religious texts and manuscripts. By 1956, the seminary's abundant holdings had outgrown the old Lenox Library, which was torn down to make way for a large, modern repository.

FROM THE TOWN TO THE UNIVERSITY

1746 1896

To observe the sesquicentennial (150th anniversary) of the College of New Jersey in October 1896, Princeton Borough erected two triumphal arches on Nassau Street. There were firework displays during the celebrations and the campus was illuminated by Chinese lanterns. During a final convocation on October 22, U.S. President Grover Cleveland spoke and college president Francis L. Patton announced that henceforth the school would have a new name—Princeton University.

This aerial view of Princeton's central campus shows the university's pleasing mix of architectural styles. Most of the dormitories and classrooms are in the Gothic Revival style favored during a wave of building in the late nineteenth and early twentieth centuries, such as the connected Chancellor Greene Library and Pyne Hall (upper left). But the school's oldest building, Nassau Hall (center), is more in the Georgian style. Stanhope Hall (center right) and the former dormitory of West College (far right, center) reflect Federalist influences. Whig and Clio Halls (upper right) were completed in 1893, replacing 1838 buildings. These Greek Revival structures were purposely designed to be identical and equal, as they were used by two fiercely competitive debating societies. (Courtesy of Princeton Pictorial Archive.)

Horrors! Columbia University-style lions and not Princeton tigers once guarded Nassau Hall. The use of orange and black as Princeton colors in the 1860s led students to adopt the tiger as their mascot two decades later. The Class of 1879, which had donated these lion statues, replaced them with tigers in 1911. (Courtesy of Princeton Pictorial Archive.)

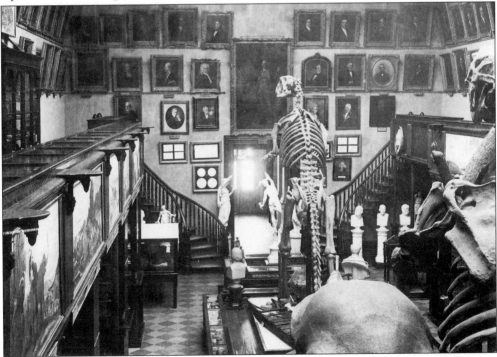

The large south central room of Nassau Hall was the college's chapel in 1756, its library in 1855, and was finally converted into its formal Faculty Room. But from 1873 to 1909, it housed a wonderful natural history museum. Benjamin Waterhouse Hawkins, the English artist who made some of the first dinosaur reconstructions, organized the museum, mounted its fossils, and created its flamboyant paintings of the "antediluvian" (prehistoric, or "pre-Flood") world.

Built in 1897, Blair Hall was among the first great Collegiate Gothic edifices erected at Princeton. Although situated at the back of campus away from Nassau Street, the dormitory's arch was a main entrance to the university because visitors were carried directly to it by the branch railroad line. In 1918, the site of the shuttle station (left) was moved a quarter mile south to make room for additional dorms.

The stained-glass-defused lighting, Venetian Gothic appointments and balustraded splendor of the Chancellor Greene Library enveloped Princeton's books in 1873. After an 1896 expansion, this delightful building was retained as a reading room, and in 1947, when the immense Firestone Library was built, it was wisely adapted for new use as a student center.

This charming harplike stairwell feature is from the Class of 1879 Hall. The skill and strength of Italian, Welsh, and Scottish stonemasons contributed to the university's beauty.

Though many of the stonemasons were from overseas, much of the stone used to build the university was local, extracted from Margerum's Quarry (now the site of Quarry Park near Harrison Street). One building contractor, the Thompson-Starrett Company of New York, used this fearsome equipment to cut the slabs.

Freshman were mercilessly harassed by sophomore hazing committees, like these Hogarth-style dissolutes from the Class of 1891. In the late 1860s, the "froshes" were enjoined from the gentlemanly fashion of carrying a cane. Cane-snatching "sprees" (riots) followed. These were ended in 1876 by the institution of regulated contests in which the object was to wrest a cane from the opponent's grasp.

Founded in 1883, the Princeton College Dramatic Association was renamed the Triangle Club a decade later (in part because the triangle is a semi-musical instrument and the club produced semi-musicals). Triangle's tradition of drag roles began with its first production *The Honorable Julius Caesar*. Co-author and future American literary figure Booth Tarkington portrayed the lean and hungry Cassius.

Confidently brushing his mortarboard, this student is dressed in 1902 for matriculative success. Then as now, attractive pinups share wall space with general artwork.

While students study and play, a huge support system labors behind the scenes. This massive nineteenth-century boiler system helped keep Princeton's stone buildings warm.

Univ. Boat House
Princeton

Crew was organized at Princeton in 1870, but for nearly thirty-five years the nearby Delaware & Raritan Canal was where the rowers trained and their boathouse stood (above). Dodging canal vessels provided experience in steering, but the crews yearned for open water to host meets. Andrew Carnegie provided it.

Carnegie Lake was first called "Loch Carnegie" to doubly honor the Scottish-born industrialist-philanthropist who funded the two-and-a-half year, $350,000 project, in which 300 acres of land were cleared and the Millstone River dammed to create three-and-a-half miles of rowing waters. Carnegie appeared at opening ceremonies on December 5, 1906, and the students sang, "Andy, Andy, you're a dandy."

Princeton class reunions started with former students returning at commencement to visit professors and see friends. By 1896, classes were marching in a parade to the Princeton-Yale baseball game held the Saturday before commencement. This "P-rade" has evolved into a grand procession, with major reunions donning elaborate costumes. (Note: Members of the Class of 1908 are portraying circus performers, not Harvard men.)

Palmer Stadium was one of America's first collegiate football stadiums. The gift of Edgar Palmer, Class of 1903, in memory of his father Stephen, the 45,000-seat structure was constructed in 1913–14 using the then-novel technology of reinforced concrete. It saw many thrilling gridiron duels and track meets, but decades of weathering finally took their toll and in 1997 the venerable venue was demolished to make way for a new stadium.

Princeton does not invite keynote speakers to its graduations. Instead, the university's president offers remarks. But tradition was broken for the school's 200th anniversary, and on June 17, 1947, Harry Truman, the President of the United States (center left, with glasses), gave the commencement address. Also in attendance was former President Herbert Hoover (below Truman).

Four
An International Community

Princeton youths of English, Irish, Italian, and African descent enjoy smiling summer camaraderie in July 1950. For decades, a melange of ethnic groups has culturally enriched the town. (Arthur Van Horn photo, courtesy of Princeton Pictorial Archive.)

Where Many Nations Dwell

The presence of several major institutions of higher learning plus the tremendous growth of the U.S. One business corridor, with its busy office parks populated by both multinational corporations and small entrepreneurial startup ventures, today make Princeton a truly international community. Drawn by educational or work opportunities, numerous nationalities and virtually every race, color, and creed live, work, play, and worship here. But as with so much about Princeton, the more things change the more they remain the same. Princeton has exhibited a vibrant diversity for many, many years.

As a British colony, many early settlers of New Jersey, including Princeton, were of English and Scottish descent. But there was a strong dose of Dutch presence in the region, a legacy of the early-seventeenth-century colonization of nearby New Amsterdam (New York) by Holland. The Scots had an important presence in Princeton, many drawn in the eighteenth century by opportunities in America. After the English and Scots, the Irish became a predominant immigrant group in Princeton in the first half of the nineteenth century. Irish labor was largely responsible for the construction of the Delaware & Raritan Canal, but the Irish also settled in Princeton to work at many other tasks. In the late 1800s, Italians from the countryside northeast of Naples found employment in the nearby Rocky Hill quarry. Rockingham, the country house which had been Washington's final headquarters, was used as a boarding house for these workers. Out of respect for the father of their adopted country, these laborers kept the room once occupied by Washington clean and unoccupied. By the late 1800s and early 1900s, immigrants from Molise in central Italy and Ischia in the Bay of Naples found employment during the great building boom on the university campus, either in local quarries or on construction crews. Landscaping and the creation of Lake Carnegie also provided employment for Italian immigrants. Such was their presence that in 1908 New Street was renamed Humbert Street in honor of King Umberto of Italy, and by 1920 Oakland Street was called "Little Italy."

Princeton's African-American community was long thought to have been founded by slaves sent North to wait upon young white Southern gentlemen studying at Princeton prior to the Civil War. But recent research has indicated that such arrangements were banned by the school. Many slaves were freed under New Jersey's 1804 Gradual Abolition of Slavery Act (men at age twenty-five, women at twenty-one), and African Americans were able to find some general employment opportunities in town. Like European immigrants, they soon had entrepreneurs and business owners among their numbers.

Although individual Jews appear to have lived briefly in Princeton in the nineteenth century, the town's present Jewish community traces its beginnings to Louis Kaplan, who moved to town in 1910. The community grew slowly and for many years its members commuted via trolley or auto to Trenton for religious services and kosher foods. By 1930, there were about twenty-five Jewish families in Princeton successfully engaged in a variety of trades. Their numbers increased in the mid-1930s with the arrival of refugees fleeing the deteriorating European political situation—the most famous of whom was of course Albert Einstein—and the establishment in the 1940s of nearby research facilities, which drew scientists and engineers of many different religious and ethnic backgrounds.

Many of the European intellectual émigrés from France, Germany, and other European countries who fled Nazism in the 1930s and 1940s enjoyed Princeton's lovely environs and continental qualities, but were dismayed to find racial segregation in movie theaters and elementary schools. Also, the wives of male European professors were not welcomed to use the research facilities at all-male Princeton (nor at most other American universities) even though many of these women held high academic degrees themselves and had been noted scholars in their native lands. Of course, Princetonians now freely and fully work, study, and play together.

Japanese and Chinese students attended Princeton University in the nineteenth century, but the town did not have a significant Asian population until the post-World War II research and development boom drew engineers from Asia to the region. Hispanic immigrants, many from Central America, are now making Princeton their home. If history is any guide, these latest arrivals will swell the ranks of community and business leaders and advance Princeton's international profile into the twenty-first century.

James MacDonald, a Scottish gardener, lived with his wife on the site of what is now Springdale Golf Course near Alexander Road. Here they are seated with their clan of children and grandchildren behind a family home at 160 Mercer Street. Unlike many of Princeton's Scots, who were Presbyterians, the MacDonalds were Baptists who later joined the Methodist Church.

James Vandeventer, born around 1800, poses for the camera *c.* 1890. His family's tree and plant nursery lent its name to present-day Vandeventer Street. Dutch farmers settled much of central New Jersey, in particular Montgomery Township just north of Princeton.

The Dorothea's House Girls Club sits for a group portrait around 1920. The center was endowed in 1914 by Dr. Guy Richard McLane in memory of his wife Dorothea, who was devoted to the Italian community and wished its young people to have a place for social activities during their first years in town. Dorothea's House is now home to several YM/YWCA programs.

Poised for berry picking in 1898 are (from left to right) Henry Brehmeyer, Elizabeth Hetzer, Lena Brehmeyer Kurkjian, Dora Brehmeyer Ufert, and August Brehmeyer. Elizabeth was a cousin to the others, who were siblings. All were Swiss immigrants who worked in Paterson's booming silk mills before moving south to Princeton. Elizabeth and Dora married Germans, and Lena married Krikor Kurkjian, an Armenian on whose Cherry Valley Road farm this photo was taken. Kurkjian first sold his produce in nearby Rocky Hill, then from a store at 2 Nassau Street in Princeton. The latter site became home to a Ford Motor Company agency and garage, which Kurkjian operated.

The bugle corps of the Charles W. Robinson Post No. 218 of the American Legion makes a gallant sight in 1915. Separate white and black American Legion and Veterans of Foreign Wars (VFW) posts were established in Princeton, but participated in joint Memorial Day parades and other patriotic observances.

Albert Einstein gave the last of his annual opening addresses for the local United Jewish Appeal fund drive at this Princeton Inn dinner in 1954, the year before his death. To Einstein's left are Princeton professor Thomas Stix, women's division chair Nora Greenblatt, and Dr. Henry Abrams, Einstein's eye doctor, who chauffeured the elderly physicist to UJA events. (Courtesy of Robert Landau.)

Volunteers and passersby at the Garden Club of Princeton's 1951 flower sale at the French Market on Nassau Street and University Place seem fascinated by a fez-wearing gentleman who has stopped to purchase some blooms. Princeton University, the Institute for Advanced Study, the Princeton Theological Seminary, and other institutions continue to attract a multitude of foreign scholars and visitors, making Princeton an even more international community.

Five
Homes Humble and Grand

A modest, sunlight-dappled house on a shady street is quintessentially Princeton. This residence at 36 Mercer Street is also typical of the work of Charles Steadman, a carpenter-builder whose structures changed the face of Princeton in the nineteenth century. (Photo by Constance M. Greiff.)

In the Dwelling Places

"Princeton is idyllic. It is buried in verdure," rhapsodized Cesar Pronier, a Swiss professor of theology who visited the town in September 1873. "The streets are simply roads bounded by beautiful trees and broad sidewalks. Each house is separated from its neighbor by a large plot of land. . . . The house is never next to the road. A garden, sometimes rather large, separates them. . . . The village is not a block of houses, but a vast space where one sees charming villas spread out. It's pretty, delightful even."

Pronier eloquently records one of the dominant images of Princeton as a village which is not only situated in the countryside, but seems to have incorporated that countryside within in its very boundaries. As architectural historian Constance M. Greiff has noted, a slightly different (but no less picturesque) vision of Princeton evolved from 1850 to World War II, that of "a quiet college town ringed by gentlemen's country estates." But there have been other realities to Princeton domiciles: from the once-active hotel trade that was a legacy of the stagecoach era to the shelters of the less affluent citizens. Hence this chapter is called "Homes Humble and Grand."

The best surviving examples of eighteenth- and early-nineteenth-century Princeton buildings are brick Georgian- or Federal-style structures, although the town was certainly filled once with more humble wooden homes. A few seventeenth-century houses, such as The Barracks (page 15), were made of local field stone.

Then came Massachusetts-born Charles Steadman (1790–1868), a carpenter and builder-architect who profoundly influenced the town's appearance. Steadman, who was also Princeton's first real estate developer, mixed Federal and Greek Revival stylings in his structures. These included the first Princeton Bank building, the First Presbyterian Church, Miller Chapel at the Princeton Theological Seminary, the former borough hall at 50 Stockton Street, and numerous homes within the Stockton-Mercer-Edgehill Streets triangle and down adjacent Alexander Street. The original section of Drumthwacket, the mansion at 344 Stockton Street (see below), may have been a Steadman project. As architectural historian Greiff puts it: "Steadman transformed Princeton from a Delaware Valley village of brick and stone to a New England-style town of wood and decorous classicism."

Another major shaper of Princeton environs was architect Rolf W. Bauhan (1892)–1966), who designed more than seventy local buildings and is credited with renovations or additions to one hundred and fifty more. Although Bauhan at times designed structures in Tudor and Norman revival styles, his predominant work in

Colonial Revival helped reinforce Princeton's eighteenth-century atmosphere.

First among Princeton estates in terms of historical interest is Morven (page 13), long the home of the Stocktons and from 1954 to 1978, the home of New Jersey's governors. Other signers of the Declaration of Independence are associated with Princeton houses: Maybury Hill on Snowden Lane was the boyhood home of Joseph Hewes; and Tusculum, on what is now Cherry Hill Road, was the farm of John Witherspoon, which he built in 1773 and where he devoted himself in his final years to farming experiments. Witherspoon rented out Tusculum at one point but in a newspaper advertisement stressed: "The Proprietor being fond of agriculture and engaged in a scheme of improvement, will not let any of the land for tillage."

A lovely home at 15 Hodge Road was built in 1854 as a gift from Commodore Richard F. Stockton to his daughter Caroline Stockton Dod and her husband. Former U.S. President Grover Cleveland purchased the property in 1896, undertook extensive renovations, renamed it "Westland" in honor of his friend Dean Andrew Fleming West, and lived there until his death in 1908.

Princeton's grandest estate was certainly Drumthwacket. (Its Gaelic name, meaning "wooded hill," was taken from a site in a Sir Walter Scott novel.) Situated just west of town on Stockton Street (Route 206), the estate was originally owned by businessman and Civil War-era governor Charles Smith Olden, who had its mansion constructed in 1834–35. The 48-acre property was purchased in 1893 by Moses Taylor Pyne, who doubled the mansion's size and added nearly 250 adjoining acres to the estate. The grounds behind Drumthwacket were exquisitely landscaped with plantings, ponds, and arched bridges. Pyne, whose fondness for Tudor Revival architecture survives in the Lower Pyne building at Nassau and Witherspoon, caused great Elizabethan-style gardeners' and farmers' homes to be erected at the back of his property. These magnificent and immediately recognizable outbuildings–mansions in their own rights–survive on what are now separate land parcels along Mercer Road. Drumthwacket was acquired by the state in the 1970s to serve as the governor's residence when it became clear that Morven was too small for official functions.

Mansions and estates alone did not cause the town's expansion, although some of the developments rising in former farm fields were certainly grand: for example, around 1907 the ubiquitous Moses Taylor Pyne (whose profound influence on town and campus architecture through the many projects he facilitated has already been noted) funded new faculty housing on Fitzrandolph and Broadmead. Because of the predominance of white stucco, the project was called "White City." Mail-order houses by Lewis Homes became popular as Jefferson Road and surrounding streets became developed just before the Depression.

After purchasing Drumthwacket, Moses Taylor Pyne (facing camera) not only enlarged its mansion, but also its grounds. Here he relaxes in one of the beautifully landscaped gardens on his estate.

William Southard's wood and coal yard at 126 Witherspoon, *c.* 1896, makes up half of this residential/retail combination.

High Victorian, with Italianate window headings and a French mansard roof topped with Gothic cast-iron pinnacles, reigns triumphant at the home of George Goldie on University Place. Goldie, a Scotsman, was Princeton University's first athletic director.

Commanding a fine view (or "prospect") of the lowland south of town, Prospect House is one of the finest surviving examples of Victorian Italianate architecture. Completed in 1852 for Thomas F. Potter, a wealthy Delaware & Raritan Canal stockholder, it became part of the university in 1877 and for ninety-one years housed its presidents. Its gardens are even more elegant today than when this 1897 photograph was taken.

Princeton's reputation as being populated by well-educated professionals is supported by this well-appointed home library.

More familial but similarly dignified is the parlor of the Redding family on Washington Road, shown in 1898. John Redding was overseer of the university's heating plant.

The University Hotel, designed by prominent architect William A. Potter, was a busy Nassau Street establishment when visited by this coach-and-four in 1878. It boasted more than one hundred rooms and saw its share of great gatherings, but could not stay in business. After use as a dormitory, it was torn down in June 1916. The dining rooms of Rockefeller College now occupy the site. (Courtesy of Princeton Pictorial Archive.)

The Central Hotel at 5 Witherspoon Street featured Franz Hill's imported German beer. But this address became the local destination for French cuisine, first as the Dupraz Hotel and currently as Lahiere's Restaurant.

Wopowog was an elegant Tudor Revival mansion at the corner of Hodge Road and Library Place. Built in 1903 for stockbroker Alexander Hudnut and his wife Belle, it was torn down in 1937 after a fire. Library Place (which runs past the library of the nearby Princeton Theological Seminary) is perhaps the town's most elegant address.

Baker Street ran south from Hulfish and emptied onto Nassau via Baker's Alley. The Baker Street neighborhood was torn down in 1935 for the construction of Palmer Square. The developers worked successfully to find its residents new housing. Several homes on the right of this picture were saved and moved to Birch Avenue.

Walk along Wiggins Street and look north on Jefferson Road. Today you will see a tree-shaded street filled with cozy two-story houses. But when this picture was taken, some time after 1911, you would have seen open skies and the first houses springing up from former corn fields.

Having originally graced a Philadelphia residence designed in 1836 by Thomas Ustick Walter (architect of the U.S. Capitol's dome), these stately Ionic columns were moved to Princeton around 1900 for use in the Mercer Manor. When the mansion was demolished in 1957, the columns again survived and were moved across Mercer Street (Princeton Pike) to become a monument at the Princeton Battlefield Park. On sunny summer days, the former portico is a popular backdrop for wedding party photos.

This is the humble home of a grand man. Albert Einstein enjoyed his final years in this modest residence at 112 Mercer Street. At his request, it was neither turned into a museum nor opened to the public. Remember a brilliant and kindly person as you view its exterior, but respect the privacy of its present inhabitants, just as Einstein's privacy was respected by his fellow Princetonians.

Six

Getting About

Motorcars did not immediately vanquish practical horse-drawn transportation, as Mrs. William Townsend White of Hilltop Farm could attest in 1925. Mrs. White (nee Augusta Henrietta Roebling of the famous Trenton-based Roebling family that built the Brooklyn Bridge), opens our chapter on the varied means Princetonians have used to put the miles behind them.

What is now the main thoroughfare of Nassau Street was once part of a busy stagecoach route which helped link New York and Philadelphia. These passengers leaving the old Princeton Inn (on the site of today's borough hall) are reliving history, having hired this coach as a colorful shuttle to a Princeton University football game.

Ralph H. Peabody of Mt. Lucas Road was in evening dress when this picture was taken, but he wore more practical garb when delivering the mail by horse between nearby Griggstown and Ten Mile Run. He also kept chickens, which, he confessed, he loved for their eggs, but hated for their messes.

Edward Smalley's stage ran between Princeton and Rocky Hill, then a bustling community of light industries. Children attending Princeton High School commuted via the coach, which of necessity in winter was this sturdy sleigh.

Many Princetonians were given their final transportation by the hearse of J.D. Laurence, whose funeral parlor was located at 211–213 Nassau Street.

This snapshot, taken during an April 1910 picnic along the Delaware & Raritan Canal, provides a rare image of a mule team of the type used to tow barges (giving the name "tow path" to the walkway along the canal). The 66-mile waterway connecting the Delaware and Raritan Rivers, built between 1830 and 1834, is now a state park.

Self-powered vessels also plied the canal, such as the freight hauler "Lottie B" seen in 1901. The Steamboat Hotel (background) has vanished, as have virtually all traces of the once-vibrant mercantile center at Princeton Basin near lower Alexander Road (then known as Canal Street).

A passenger train of the Camden & Amboy Railroad (later the Pennsylvania Railroad) crosses the canal bridge in the 1860s. The railroad reached Princeton in 1839, eventually displacing the canal's freight shipping functions. By 1866, the main rail line had been moved out to Princeton Junction and a branch line into town was established.

After Ed Kopp's 1903 Oldsmobile became one of the first autos in Princeton, cars began coexisting with pedestrians, cyclists, and horse-drawn carriages, as seen in this westward view of Nassau Street. The thoroughfare has been reinforced with gravel but is still not paved. The first coating of "asphaltum" did not come until 1916.

A slightly later view looking east shows that parking has been arranged on a diagonal, something that would be quite impossible with today's larger vehicles and much heavier traffic.

Mrs. Howard Crosby (Katherine) Warren was president of the prestigious Present Day Club in 1909–1910, and her husband was of one of Princeton University's first psychology professors. She is seen here leaving their Library Place home in style.

By 1916, Smalley's stagecoach (see page 77) had been upgraded from hay to gasoline power. Note that the back wheels of this great Packard bus are driven not by differential gears, but via an old-fashioned chain drive.

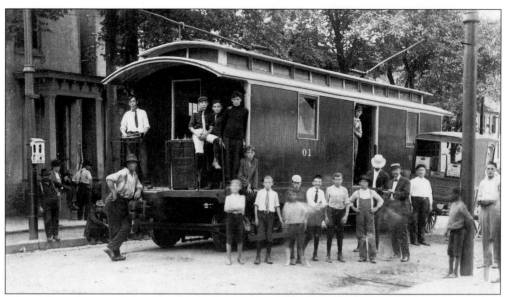

Almost forgotten are the trolley lines that once ran between Trenton and Princeton. The New Jersey and Pennsylvania Traction Co. and the Johnson Line shuttled not only passengers but goods (as witness to this trolley freight car). The tracks ran from Trenton through Lawrenceville, entered Princeton through Bayard Lane, across Mountain Avenue, and along Witherspoon as far as Spring Street. Service was discontinued around 1942.

Bicycles keep rolling as a mode of transportation for many Princetonians. Mary Dohm of 36 University Place is seated on a old-fashioned bike which, except for its rudimentary gear system, might hold its own with the rugged wheels favored for today's town riding.

For Princeton student Hobart Baker (shown here with friend Rolf Bauhan, right), motorcycling was just one more sport to master. This godlike athlete could rival golf and tennis professionals and exploded with spectacular hockey skating drives that elicited cries of "Here he comes!" A Lafayette Escadrille squadron commander in World War I, he died in a 1918 plane crash. The university's skating rink is named in his memory.

In 1917 Major James Barnes, Princeton Class of 1893, and Marshall Mills, Class of 1902, founded the Princeton Flying School to meet the need for fighter pilots. The school trained at an airfield located off Princeton Pike before its functions were officially assumed by the Army. One graduate, George Vaughan, age nineteen, was a top World War I ace.

John Bancroft assisted generations of commuters on the "Dinky," the shuttle train on the 2-mile "PJ&B" ("Princeton Junction and Back") branch line into Princeton. The beloved conductor holds a sign of his service, received as a momento when he retired in July 1978. (Photo by Jeff Macechak, courtesy of Princeton Pictorial Archive.)

Seven

Life and Leisure

Outfitted in stout clothing and toting walking sticks, bags, and guide books, the women's tourist club is poised in 1890 for broadening and improving adventures. Princetonians have long enjoyed active lifestyles.

Families, Fun, and Volunteerism

The soul of a town is its religious institutions and commerce its sinews. But its heart beats in community activities. The best of Princeton has been expressed over the years in its family leisure time and its volunteer pursuits.

Sports are a major part of the local lifestyle, with athletic traditions going back long before the tennis, basketball, and soccer games contested in modern Princeton parks. For example, a diary written by a College of New Jersey student in 1786 records that he played at "base ball." (This information has helped support claims that the game was well known in America before its supposed invention in Cooperstown, New York, by Abner Doubleday in the 1830s.) Princeton University's role in the establishment of American college football and track and field in the nineteenth century is well documented. In addition to these pastimes, university baseball and crew became popular spectator sports among townspeople. Meanwhile, active sports clubs were established in town.

Winter sports hold a special place in town memory. Skaters frequented Carnegie Lake (and afterwards, Renwick's or The Balt for hot chocolate). For many years, flags were placed in a tree in front of the Lower Pyne building at Nassau and Witherspoon advising whether the lake ice was safe for skating (white for solid and safe, red for thin and dangerous). This lovely community tradition ended, however, in the 1960s.

Theatres have enlivened the local scene. Thompson Hall, which hosted amateur theatrics, dances, and other diversions, and the Arcade, a small movie house, are now both gone; so is the Princeton Playhouse, once the town's largest cinema. But still alight is the Garden Theatre, whose history stretches back to vaudeville days and whose name comes from its location on the former garden next to Bainbridge House at the corner of Nassau and Vandeventer. The Princeton Community Players, an amateur theatre group, was founded in 1933 and later jointly staged musical comedies with the P.J. & B. Players (a group formed by friendly commuters on the "Princeton Junction and Back" shuttle train). Today, amateur theatrics, dance, instrumental and vocal music, and the fine arts are further championed by the Arts Council of Princeton.

Local arts have of course been tremendously boosted by the presence of Princeton University. The school's Triangle Club opened McCarter Theatre in 1930. The venue was not merely a showcase for Triangle's witty and occasionally wacky annual musicals (featuring the all-male kick line traditionally written into every show); it quickly became a nationally renowned stage, premiering works by playwrights as diverse as

Thorton Wilder and Clare Booth Luce. For a time, McCarter was also a popular stage for previews of Broadway-bound productions. The university took over the building in 1950, and in 1970 McCarter officially became an independent theater. Its reputation continues to grow. So does that of the university's art museum. Its collection of ancient art benefited in the 1920s and 1930s from the success of expeditions to Greco-Roman archeological sites. In recent years, alumni have enriched its holdings with donations of fabulous examples American, Asian, African, and European works.

Lodges, clubs, and societies have flourished in Princeton. In 1763 a petition was granted establishing the "St. John's Lodge" of the Freemasons in Princeton. The local Mason chapters came and went until the 1856 establishment of Princeton Lodge Number 38. The Nassau Club was organized in 1895, originally for men, and the Present Day Club three years later for women. Volunteerism in Princeton has, paradoxically, reached almost professional levels. No better example is the borough's firefighting organizations. The Princeton Fire Company was established in 1788, and in 1847 Mercer Engine Company No. 3 came into being. The demands of the Civil War for soldiers drained the community of able-bodied firefighters and the two companies nearly disbanded. But in 1865, as the war concluded, the two groups were not only reorganized, but a third entity, a hook and ladder company, was established. Thanks to effective volunteer fire companies, Princeton has never experienced a devastating town-wide conflagration, a major factor in the wonderful preservation of centuries of local architecture.

Ironically, an international medical crisis led directly to the establishment of one of Princeton's most important institutions—and, by extension, the spirit of community support that benefits so many others. The terrible influenza pandemic of 1918–1919 did not spare Princeton, and necessitated a makeshift hospital to handle local cases of what proved an often deadly illness. The following year, money was raised for a permanent hospital, established that November on the former Grover farm at the far end of Witherspoon Street. (Although modern buildings have superseded the old there, the site of the Medical Center at Princeton remains the same.) The June Hospital Fete (pronounced "fett"), an annual country fair with entertainment, auctions, and music and athletic competitions, serves as an important fund-raiser and outreach event for the hospital. Such successful fund-raising and community involvement is as characteristic of Princeton life as anything.

The Jesse Lynch Williams family typifies the ideal domestic bliss of an early-twentieth-century family. Williams was a Pulitzer Prize-winning playwright.

No less charming and content is this unidentified family, dressed in their Sunday finery and gathered on their porch somewhere in the Baker Street or Witherspoon Street districts.

Thanksgiving was the major costume holiday for American children before Halloween took hold, as seen in these Pilgrims and Indians *c*. 1909. Note that little Native Americans outnumber little Europeans 24 to 4; an accurate reflection of early-seventeenth-century demographics, perhaps, but probably indicative of which group was more appealing to portray.

Oh, to have had this photo in color! These high-fashion ladies, wives of the Princeton Class of 1882, were entertained in 1902 by Mrs. John G. Hibben (seated front row and far right) while their husbands attended class reunions.

As the nearby Delaware & Raritan Canal declined in importance as a shipping artery with the ascendancy of the railroads, early trends foreshadowed its present use as a state park. Here some children transform one of the canal locks into a swimming hole.

The rugged "Olympic" football team featured substance over style. Unable to afford special uniforms, they chalk-marked O's on their sweaters and did quite well.

Further evidence of Princetonians' love of sports (and sporting fashionably functional short haircuts) is the 1926 high school girls' basketball team.

In the 1890s—long before the 1960s hootenanny craze—making music on the guitar, 5-string banjo, and mandolin was a popular pastime. The Jared Wolfe family enthuses over plucked string cheer while gathered at the Beatty House, 19 Vandeventer Avenue.

The powdered wig and gown-bedecked elegance of an eighteenth-century ball at Morven was recreated in 1901 during what was erroneously believed to be the mansion's 200th Christmas. Among the revelers hosted by then-owner Dr. Charles Woodruff Shields (seated, center) were numerous descendants of Richard and Annis Boudinot Stockton, Morven's first owners.

Performing at a local Elks club are drummer Mike Meyers, a pianist believed to be Alma Lambert (mother of Princeton-born stride piano great Donald Lambert), an unidentified violinist (possibly George Jordan), and an unknown trumpet player. This combo easily predates 1935, the year the Benny Goodman Trio was heralded as the first integrated jazz combo to perform in public.

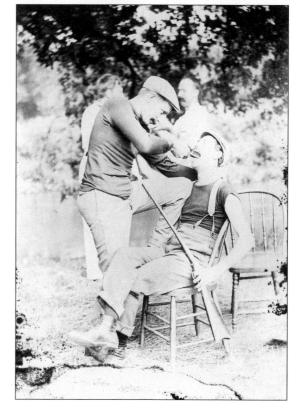

Two unidentified men enjoy an outing by a local river and demonstrate budget dentistry. But isn't there a molar nerve that connects directly to the trigger finger?

The Princeton Municipal Band marches in a Nassau Street parade. Community bands were popular at the turn of the century, and many American small towns had them. (Courtesy of Princeton Pictorial Archive.)

The Princeton Fire Company was organized on February 18, 1788. As the town grew, so did its needs for efficient fire fighting. Mercer Engine Company No. 3 was founded in 1847. Members pose at their Chambers Street headquarters sometime before 1923.

John F. Huff, foreman of Mercer Engine Company No. 3, proudly displays the uniform and symbolic horn of his office.

Princeton University students training with the Army Signal Corps to become fliers during World War I (see page 83) also did ground level drills. The terrible and costly conflict led to the creation in Nassau Hall's entry of a memorial to Princeton's war dead. (Courtesy of Princeton Pictorial Archive.)

During World War II, volunteer plane spotters from town and campus kept watching the skies in case enemy craft flew over New Jersey from the Atlantic. The "Princeton Listening Post" at the university also monitored Nazi English-language short wave radio propaganda broadcasts. (Courtesy of Princeton Pictorial Archive.)

A magnificent monument to George Washington's victory at the Battle of Princeton was erected near the intersections of Bayard Lane and Stockton Street. Its dedication on June 9, 1922, attracted no less a speaker than President Warren G. Harding, shown on the podium addressing the assemblage.

Princeton Borough's finest pose stalwartly in the late 1930s. The force included Sgt. Phillip Diggs, the town's first African-American policeman (seated far right). (Courtesy of Princeton Pictorial Archive.)

This late 1940s YMCA banquet was one of many local events held to strengthen ties between fathers and sons throughout the community.

The ladies auxiliary of Princeton's black YMCA holds a Valentine's Day tea in 1944. Such events raised morale and community spirit while so many men were off fighting during World War II. (Courtesy of Mrs. Martha Barbour.)

One bartender at the Annex Grill (left) bet on incumbent president Harry S. Truman, while another (right) bet on challenger Thomas E. Dewey. The payoff of a merry post-election wheelbarrow ride was once a common sight in America. But the 1948 vote was no laughing matter for famed Princeton-based opinion poller George Gallup who, like most of his colleagues, had incorrectly forecast a Dewey victory.

In the mid-1950s, the main hall of the then-new Jewish Center of Princeton did double service as the site of Saturday worship and a Sunday morning religious school. Subsequent expansion at the center gave the sanctuary and classrooms their own spaces. (Courtesy of The Jewish Center of Princeton.)

Who could better represent Princeton life than such gregarious champions of a worthy cause? These boosters for a 1960s Princeton Country Day school fair typify the spirit of local school fund-raisers, the famous June "Hospital Fete" for the Medical Center at Princeton, and numerous other activities benefiting community endeavors.

Eight

Worship

The Baronness Hyde de Neuville (c. 1779–1849) sketched "Princeton's Church" on October 27, 1813. This is apparently the Nassau Street Presbyterian Church after the first of two major fires that destroyed it. From the Quaker and Presbyterian foundations of its worship, the town has grown to embrace a variety of faiths.

To the Greater Glory

As noted earlier, the first major settlement in the area was at Stony Brook, site of the Stony Brook Meeting of the Society of Friends (Quakers). The first meetinghouse, built in 1726, was rebuilt in 1760 after a fire. This stone building still stands. The Princeton-area meeting was "laid down" in 1878 as many descendants of the original Quakers began to embrace Presbyterian or Episcopalian worship. It was revived in 1941 during renewed interest in Quakerism and remains active today, now also having an affiliated grade school.

The town's first Presbyterian congregation was organized in 1755. The First Presbyterian Church building itself was started in 1762 and finished four years later. During the interim, the congregation worshiped at the chapel of the College of New Jersey or else attended services at existing churches in Lawrenceville or Kingston. Like many Princeton buildings, the original Presbyterian Church was occupied and ill-used by troops during the Revolution, first the British and then the Americans. Because so many of the local people were adherents to this domination, by 1847, a Second Presbyterian Church was organized and its first building completed in 1850.

The Episcopal church soon became a presence in town. Its first congregation was formed and its first house of worship constructed in 1833. The present Trinity Episcopal Church has had three major fires since the core building was constructed in 1868, but these disasters have only been the catalyst for rebuilding and beautiful enlargement. An Episcopal chapel once stood near the canal turning basin near Alexander Street (then known as Canal Street). Originally a mission of Trinity Church to the residents and visitors associated with the active waterway, services and Sunday school were held there into the 1900s, well after the canal lost importance.

A Methodist Episcopal church (now known simply as the Methodist church) was erected in 1847 and rebuilt in 1866 and again in 1906.

In the second quarter of the nineteenth century, Catholicism became established in town. The first Roman Catholic church was established in 1847 and was known as the Immaculate Conception Mission until the 1850s. As the African-American community grew and prospered, three leading houses of worship ministered to its members: the Witherspoon Street Presbyterian Church, the Mount Pisgah African Methodist Episcopal Church, and the Bright Hope Baptist Church.

So small was the Princeton Jewish community that for many years it lacked a minyan (the ten-worshiper minimum needed to hold services), so its members worshiped in Trenton. Then in 1926, Isadore Braveman, a watch repairer and jewelry store owner who was also a cantor, founded Congregation B'nai Zion in a rented storefront on Spring Street. During World War II, this humble center extended hospitality to Jews at the officers' training school on the university campus. (Albert Einstein was a popular lecturer.) After the war, the town's Jewish community expanded with the number of scientists and professionals hired by the RCA Sarnoff Laboratories and Heyden Chemical Corporation. In July 1950, the Jewish Center of Princeton acquired its first property on Olden Avenue, and then in 1956 established its present temple, school, and community center on upper Nassau Street.

Today there is scarcely a major religious denomination that is not represented by a house of worship either in Princeton itself (including Lutheran, Christian Science, Unitarian, United Church of Christ, and Seventh Day Adventist) or in nearby communities (including Reformed Church, Mormon, Islamic, and Jehovah's Witness).

But not all major religious observances in the region have been held indoors. Methodist revivals swept America in the late nineteenth and early twentieth centuries, and beginning in the 1890s, such meetings were held at a campground in nearby Skillman. These gatherings attracted throngs of worshippers from Princeton, as well as Rocky Hill, Kingston, Belle Mead, and as far away as Somerville and Trenton. The faithful were drawn by hearty dinners, a chance to socialize with neighbors, and, of course, the fiery, uplifting sermons of the Methodist preachers. The summertime events ended around 1930 but are immortalized in the name of Camp Meeting Avenue in Skillman.

The Friends Meeting House at Stony Brook is located near the intersection of Quaker Bridge and Mercer Roads and its exterior is shown on page 12. The nearby burial ground is the area's oldest, with the earliest graves unmarked according to early Quaker practice. "First Day" (Sunday) meetings are still held in the nearly 250-year-old structure.

The interior of the old Methodist Episcopal Church, erected in 1849 on the corner of Nassau and Vandeventer, with its filigreed ceiling decorations and semicircular pews, evokes the feeling of an ancient temple. It was torn down in 1909 to make way for the present Methodist church.

"The Bright Hope Baptist Church has a commodious building, with lecture room in the basement," wrote local black historian Anna Bustill Smith in 1913. Mrs. Smith also noted with pride that this church on John Street, the Witherspoon Presbyterian Church (where Paul Robeson's father was pastor), and the Mt. Pisgah African Methodist Episcopal Church all had "their own parsonages, electric light and steam heat."

"Cook's Hall" on upper Nassau Street, shown here in 1872, was built in 1847 as the Second Presbyterian Church.

As suggested by this photo, taken *c.* 1895, Trinity Church was richly decorated with polychrome-stenciled walls, colorful floor tiles, and intricate carvings. Designed by R.M. Upjohn (son of the architect of Trinity in New York) and built in 1868, it has retained its grandeur through several additions and rebuildings, including restoration after a major 1963 fire.

In 1926, thanks in large part to the unflagging efforts of local businessman Isadore Braveman, Congregation B'nai Zion met on the second floor of the old Branch Building on Witherspoon Street. The congregation then rented the storefront on the left of this photo, just around the corner at 9 Spring Street, before acquiring its own center. B'nai Zion provided the only place of religious gathering for Jewish students at Princeton until the university invited B'nai Brith to form a Hillel branch on campus in January 1947.

These dramatically costumed children portrayed an archangel and a knight in a Trinity Church pageant about the crusades.

Dating from 1869, "Old St. Paul's" at Nassau and Moore Streets was actually the third church built for Princeton's Roman Catholics. This view shows the new facade added in 1912. It was torn down in 1954 to make way for the present St. Paul's.

Nine

The Famous
and Influential

Woodrow Wilson (1856–1924) was an activist reformer during his years as Princeton University president and New Jersey governor. As President of the United States, he retained Princeton as his official address and returned to vote on election days at the Mercer Engine Company No. 3 firehouse on Chambers Street.

Presidents and Pollsters, Scribes and Scientists

In a sense, the many important persons who have lived in Princeton are as much a monument to the town's place in history as the Battlefield Park or Nassau Hall. But it may be more difficult for the tourist or newcomer to understand this because Princetonians have been loathe to put up memorials to their own, preferring to let their memories live on in the very air of the village.

But there are some memorials, and visitors are urged to stroll or take a weekend guided tour through the Princeton Cemetery. It is the resting place of presidents of Princeton (like John Witherspoon), a President of the United States (Grover Cleveland), and other notable figures in American history (such as Aaron Burr).

Many buried here should be famous even if they are not well remembered today. For example, the cemetery's largest tomb, quite noticeable from Witherspoon Street, is that of Clark Fisher, a naval engineer and Civil War veteran who held numerous patents and did experiments at the Brooklyn Navy Yard that demonstrated the value of petroleum as a fuel. Other notables interred here include Sara Agnes Pryor, a founder of the Daughters of the American Revolution; Canvass White, engineer on the Erie and Delaware & Raritan Canal projects; and Paul Tulane, the Princeton native who endowed Tulane University (and whose statue on his monument faces away from Princeton University, which refused to change its name in return for his largesse).

Although not his burial place, Princeton was the birthplace of perhaps the greatest all-around talent that America has ever known—Paul Robeson, who was born at 110 Witherspoon Street, the son of Rev. William D. Robeson of the Witherspoon Presbyterian Church. He was a football All-American, Phi Beta Kappa, and valedictorian at Rutgers University. He earned a law degree at Columbia University. He became an accomplished stage and screen actor. He was acclaimed by one critic as the greatest male voice of his generation, and surely there has been no one to rival his show-stopping version of "Old Man River" in the musical *Showboat*. (Robeson appeared in the original Broadway and Hollywood versions.) In his latter years, he turned his intellect and force of personality to political and civil rights activism.

Robeson is rivaled in talent perhaps only by the sheer genius of physicist Albert Einstein, arguably Princeton's most famous resident, who came to Princeton in 1933 to join the faculty of the Institute for Advanced Study and lived here until his death in

1955. Einstein had already done his major work in relativity theory, the photoelectric effect, and other areas of scientific inquiry by the time he settled in Princeton, yet his final years were productive ones. Although he labored unsuccessfully on a unified field theory to explain all the forces of the universe and struggled to reconcile himself with the new field of quantum physics, he greatly helped younger colleagues to develop their own theories and worked on behalf of war refugees, world peace, and the state of Israel.

George Kennan, author of America's containment strategy against the Soviets during the Cold War, is a resident. Ironically, so was Svetlana Alleluyeva, Stalin's daughter, who made Princeton her home for a time in the 1970s after leaving Russia. Other prominent persons have found the town a convenient base to commute via train to New York, while also making their mark in Princeton. The most notable examples have been Barney Kilgore, who revitalized two newspapers (the *Wall Street Journal* there and the *Princeton Packet* here), and Dr. George Gallup, who headed the Young & Rubicam ad agency's research department in the 1930s, but back home founded a little opinion polling side business that became the world-famous Gallup Poll.

Of course, the shady lanes of prestigious Princeton have also attracted a few shady characters. The most notorious was the late Simone "Sam the Plumber" DeCalvacante, convicted of running gambling operations in the state, who in 1976 traded his quiet life in Princeton Township for an even quieter retirement in Florida.

But the good and great predominate. Many of these have been associated with Princeton University. "Princeton in the nation's service," declared Woodrow Wilson, and indeed there have been thousands of prominent political leaders, scientists, scholars, builders, activists, and actors who have attended Old Nassau. (To name all of the university's world-famous alumni would seemingly require a volume as thick as a phone book; such a list will not be attempted here.)

Along with being home to the renowned university, it is as a mecca for twentieth-century literati that Princeton has become famed. F. Scott Fitzgerald (1896–1940) was here but briefly. (He withdrew from Princeton University in October 1917 during his senior year to enter officers' training for World War I.) But he celebrated Princeton and its environs in his writings, most notably in the autobiographical novel *This Side of Paradise*, which contains wonderful vignettes about the town in the early twentieth century from a student's perspective. Upton Sinclair wrote his Civil War novel *Manassas* and his hard-hitting expose of the meat-packing industry *The Jungle* on a farm on Ridgeview Road north of town. Bertrand Russell visited the Peacock Inn in the 1920s. T.S. Eliot lived briefly in Princeton and finished his play *The Cocktail Party* in 1948 while staying at 14 Alexander Street. Thorton Wilder lived briefly at the graduate college and his play *Our Town* premiered at McCarter Theater. Budd Schulberg, author of *What Makes Sammy Run*, lived at 343 Jefferson Road in the 1950s. Peter Benchley, author of *Jaws*, makes Princeton his home base.

Saul Bellow, Anthony Burgess, E.L. Doctorow, and Philip Roth are just a few of the famed novelists who have taught at Princeton. More recent faculty members have included award-winning poets and novelists Joyce Carol Oates and Toni Morrison, nonfiction writer John McPhee, and historian James McPherson.

Princeton's literary atmosphere might have formed even earlier than it did. Mark Twain often visited the Princeton home of a good friend, *Harpers Magazine* editor Laurence Hutton, in the late 1890s, and he nearly relocated here. "Princeton would suit me as well as Heaven," wrote Twain to Hutton, "Better, in fact, for I shouldn't care for that society up there."

Aaron Burr Jr. (1756–1836), who served as Vice President of the United States from 1801 to 1805, was the son of the second president of the College of New Jersey. (Both Burrs are buried in the town cemetery.) But the younger Burr is chiefly remembered for his bitter political rivalry with Alexander Hamilton, which ended on July 11, 1804, when Burr fatally shot his nemesis in a duel.

Medal-bedecked Caledonian (Scottish) Games champion and Edinburgh native George Goldie (1841–1920) became Princeton University's first athletic director in 1869. He instituted popular running, jumping, and throwing competitions based on the Highland model, which were soon staged by other colleges, making Goldie the father of modern American track and field.

President Grover Cleveland (1837–1908), the dapper top-hatted gent, and his beautiful wife Frances Folsom Cleveland (1864–1947), seated at center, attended a luncheon in the First Lady's honor on May 26, 1888, at Guernsey Hall, Prof. Allan Marquand's mansion. Cleveland, the only man to regain the presidency after an election defeat, attended the seminal 150th anniversary event at which the college was renamed Princeton University. The Clevelands retired to Princeton and are buried together in the town cemetery. In a memorial within the Cleveland Tower at the university's graduate school is displayed this wise sentiment from the chief executive who worked to reform civil service: "Public office is a public trust."

Paul Robeson (1898–1976), the great scholar, singer, actor, athlete, and activist, is shown in this rare snapshot during a visit to his hometown. He relaxes on the steps of 6–8 Spring Street with two friends from the Moore family, beautician-entrepreneur Christine and her child. (Courtesy of Donald Moore.)

Albert Einstein (1879–1955) has enduring appeal because we sense—correctly—that this awe-inspiring genius also possessed endearing humanity. He bore his fame patiently and in private enjoyed toy games, playing the violin, sailing, laughing with children, and (at least on this occasion) wearing fuzzy slippers. (Courtesy of Gillett Griffin.)

Thomas Mann (1875–1955), the German novelist who won the 1929 Nobel Prize for literature, also found refuge in Princeton from Nazism, living from 1938 to 1941 at what is now the Aquinas Institute at Stockton and Library Place. Mann wrote to a friend: "The landscape is parklike, well suited to walks, with amazingly beautiful trees which now, in Indian summer, glow in the most magnificent colors." (Collection of the Library of Congress.)

On the night of October 30, 1938, actor-director Orson Welles (1915–1985) became a fictional town resident by portraying a Princeton astronomy professor in a radio version of H.G. Wells' *War of the Worlds*. The realistic news bulletin-style broadcast, which had the murderous Martians landing at nearby Grovers Mill, New Jersey, caused a nationwide panic. (Collection of the Library of Congress.)

George H. Gallup (1901–1984) started a sideline business in a one-room Princeton office in 1935—a syndicated newspaper feature *America Speaks* which used scientific "sampling referendums" (opinion polls) to report on the nation's viewpoints. It grew into the famous Gallup Poll and helped make Princeton a world center for opinion research. (Courtesy of the Gallup Organization.)

Barney Kilgore (1908–1967) transformed Dow Jones and its once-struggling newspaper *The Wall Street Journal* into the financial information powerhouses they are today. Kilgore purchased the *Princeton Packet* from elderly owner Charles LaTourette in 1955 and made it a lively community newspaper whose eye-catching layout was far ahead of its time. (Courtesy of Dow Jones & Company.)

John O'Hara's dog, John O'Hara's Rolls-Royce (with vanity plates as a gift from Gov. Richard Hughes), and the novelist himself are pictured at his home on Pretty Brook Road in Princeton Township. O'Hara (1905–1970), author of *From the Terrace*, *Butterfield-8*, and *Pal Joey*, moved to the area in 1949 and spent his productive final years here. His headstone in the Princeton cemetery reads: "Better than anyone else he told the truth about his time."

J. Robert Oppenheimer (1904–1967) gained notoriety as a father of the atomic bomb and controversy when his growing concerns about nuclear weaponry and his past political connections brought him under suspicion during the Cold War. But this brilliant physicist and able administrator also had a highly productive tenure as director of the Institute for Advanced Study from 1947 to 1966. (Photo by Orren Jack Turner, courtesy of Princeton Pictorial Archives.)

Ten

Research and
Much Development

"Strange Traffic on Nassau Street," declared the *Princeton Alumni Weekly* on October 7, 1930. Actually, not so strange at all because shuffling houses has been a Princeton practice since the 1700s. Recalled one recent resident: "I came from the city, and to walk out my door and find a house in the middle of the street made a big impression on me."

The Paths of Progress

The more Princeton changes, the more it stays the same. John Witherspoon's eighteenth-century "scheme of improvement" of his land by agricultural experiments might fit right in with Princeton's twentieth-century R&D (research and development) boom. Indeed, if there is another facet we can add to the idea of Princeton—along with its fame as a crossroads of the Revolution, seat of higher learning, and genteel home of the influential—it would be Princeton as a place of research and development.

Princeton borough and township have striven to avoid the kind of tacky suburbanization that, it must be admitted, has been allowed to progress (if "progress" is the word) unchecked in some parts of the state. Yet Princeton keeps buzzing with building projects within its boundaries that seem to meld with the town's established historical and cultural contexts.

One of the most famous and significant of these was the creation of Palmer Square from 1935 to 1937. Edgar Palmer (1880–1943), a zinc magnate, financier, and Princeton alumnus who had donated Palmer Stadium to the university, formed Princeton Municipal Improvement, Inc., and between 1929 and 1935 began buying properties along and to the north of Nassau Street. The resulting urban renewal-style project—"Palmer Square"—created a complex of shops, apartments, and offices around a small village green which continues to boost Princeton's fortunes to this day. But it was not without controversy: to accommodate Palmer's rather mythical reinvention of a Colonial village, several real eighteenth-century buildings, notably the original Nassau Inn, were demolished to make way for Palmer Square. Picturesque Upper Pyne fell during the second stage of the square's development.

Palmer had beneficial foresight, however. Knowing that U.S. Route One was going to be developed outside town as a through-traffic alternative to the old Lincoln Highway (whose local segment was Nassau Street), he had a new post office built within the square so that people would have an important reason to visit town. The project also invigorated the local economy as it struggled with the aftereffects of the Depression. According to one old-timer, "The Palmer Square construction broke the back of the Depression in Princeton."

U.S. Highway One outside Princeton was opened as a turnpike in 1804 and was an important stagecoach road. But U.S. One was by no means the first important commercial traffic route in the area. The Princeton Pike runs through today's

Battlefield Park but was actually laid out well after the Battle of Princeton, around 1807, as a private toll road, which it remained until 1859. Traffic has been both a boon and a bane to the town, and controversies over it are nothing new. In 1913, state plans to extend and expand narrow, perambulating Mount Lucas Road ran into local opposition. Then Charles and L.V. Silvester—brothers, curators at Princeton University, and major Mount Lucas landowners—laid out a new route through woods and fields a few hundred yards to the west. The route was accepted and Route 206 was completed in 1915. (It was once known as "Route 31," but that designation is now given to a road that runs west of Princeton through Mercer and Hunterdon Counties.) One resident puzzled over "who'll ever use it way over there." The answer is, many people and more.

New Jersey's central location has had immense implications for the Princeton area. New Jersey is in the center of the great Megalopolis stretching from Boston down the East Coast to Washington, D.C., and Princeton is in the near-geographic center of New Jersey. Indeed, Jean Gottman, who first explored the implications of the great Northeast Seaboard in his 1961 book *Megalopolis* recognized Princeton's significance, referring to it as a "brain's town," that is, "a prestige location for highbrow intellectual and scientific activities."

In the process, Princeton has been reconfirmed as a major research location. This became particularly evident with the 1942 founding and post-World War II expansion of David Sarnoff's RCA laboratories on Route One. Under the guidance of Sarnoff, the brilliant and aggressive businessman who made the Radio Corporation of America what it is today, the laboratories perfected color television and made breakthroughs in numerous other communications fields. Many Sarnoff lab engineers moved into Princeton, further increasing the town's already considerable brain pool. When RCA developed a tract on the northeast end of town to provide housing for them, one of its streets was named Random Road because many RCA employees were working in the cutting edge field of random processes in communications networks.

On Route One, just south of RCA, one of the world's first factories was established in the late 1940s to produce peacetime supplies of the miracle drug discovered during wartime, penicillin. Just north of RCA, the Princeton Plasma Physics Laboratory (PPPL) was established as an adjunct to the university, but funded by the Department of Energy, its goal being to harness solar-style fusion reactions as a cheap, unlimited energy source and an alternative to highly radioactive nuclear fission (see page 124). PPPL at first occupied the buildings of the "Princeton Annex" of the Manhattan-based Rockefeller Institute for Medical Research, established in 1915 to study diseases in plants and animals. Princeton University converted the site into the James R. Forrestal Research Center, named after the Princeton alumnus who had served as Secretary of Defense from 1947 to 1949. Forrestal's name was later loaned to one of the first major office parks in the area, the Forrestal Center, developed in 1973 and patterned after the Stanford Industrial Park in Palo Alto, California. (Some historians of the megalopolis credit the establishment of the Forrestal Center as the true beginning of the modern Princeton-area Route One corridor boom.)

Most of the farms that once lined the highway have given way to office parks. The greatest compliment to a certain town is that commuters to these parks might actually be in nearby South Brunswick, Plainsboro, West Windsor or Lawrence Townships while at their jobs, but when asked where they work, they typically reply: "Princeton."

The structure at the corner of Nassau and Witherspoon is about to be moved so that the First National Bank of Princeton can erect a headquarters and office building.

Voila! When the five-story bank building opened for business on May 5, 1902, it had the only elevator in town.

Norman Rockwell puts the final touches on his hilarious painting of "Yankee Doodle" in the tap room of the Nassau Inn. It is one of few murals created by the popular illustrator. The hotel was constructed in the late 1930s to provide badly needed rooms after several establishments—including the original Colonial-era Nassau Inn—had been torn down or converted to other uses.

Like Albert Einstein, John von Neumann was a prominent European mathematician-scientist. He joined the Princeton University faculty in 1930 and three years later joined the Institute for Advanced Study. His interest in applied mathematics led him to develop one of the first supercomputers. This early model, c. 1945, was used by the U.S. Weather Bureau to predict weather patterns. (Courtesy of Princeton Pictorial Archive.)

In 1951, Princeton University astrophysicist Lyman Spitzer convinced the government to fund the Princeton Plasma Physics Laboratory and begin work on harnessing solar-style fusion reactions as an energy alternative to highly radioactive nuclear fission. PPPL's first experimental unit was the small Model A Stellarator. A smiling Spitzer posed with the once top-secret device in 1983 before its donation to the Smithsonian. (Courtesy of Princeton Plasma Physics Laboratory.)

The "Jersey" median divider, developed in the state, has prevented thousands of highway deaths by blocking and funneling cars away from head-on collisions. These dividers were installed on Route One near Princeton in the late 1950s. A series of jughandle intersections were also added at the time to make turns safer as traffic volume increased.

Just south of Route One in nearby Plainsboro, was Industrial Research Laboratories, a joint venture of AMF, RCA, Corning Glass, and seven other corporations. The futuristic dome contained the world's first privately-owned nuclear reactor to be used exclusively for research. It operated from 1959 until it was shut down in 1970.

This sequence shows the completion of Palmer Square three decades after it was begun. On July 9, 1963, Tudor Revival-style Upper Pyne, fronting on Nassau Street, is still seen on its western exposure.

By November 13, 1963, Upper Pyne is gone and with its exterior wall, the last traces of Baker's Alley, which had been eliminated during the first phase of construction on Palmer Square. The superstructure of One Palmer Square rises.

Just as the Depression had temporarily delayed the Palmer Square project, World War II delayed completion of its southeastern corner. On March 13, 1964, the new building has risen above (and, in some residents' opinion, overpowered) the quaint townscape designed in the 1920s by Thomas Stapleton, Edgar Palmer's architect.

By November 10, 1964, the job is essentially finished. Stapleton's plan had called for all Colonial Revival buildings, but this large office and retail structure was substituted to complete the square. (Photos by Eric Baker Contractors Photo Service, courtesy of Princeton Pictorial Archive.)

Around 1963, it was decided that the corner of Washington and Prospect was the ideal location for the new Woodrow Wilson School of International Studies. The problem: the old Wilson school (now Corwin Hall) already stood there. So in an engineering feat that crowned the history of Princeton house moving, the entire Corwin building was lifted off its foundations and rolled back 75 yards on a rail system.

The Woodrow Wilson School is pictured here around the time of its 1965 dedication by U.S. President Lyndon Johnson, with relocated Corwin in the background. Hearkening to an historic past and quite ready to enter the twenty-first century, the Wilson school is much like the town in which it stands.